ALBERT EINSTEIN

BOOK FOR CURIOUS KIDS

Explore the Life and Ideas of
the Legendary Scientist

MARK LYLANI

TABLE OF CONTENTS

INTRODUCTION

Have you ever gazed up at the stars and wondered about the mysteries of the universe? Have you ever dreamed of traveling through time or unlocking the secrets of light and energy? Join me on a captivating journey through the life and discoveries of one of history's greatest minds—Albert Einstein.

In this book, we'll delve into the fascinating story of Albert Einstein, a curious and imaginative boy who grew up to become a revolutionary scientist. Born in the small German city of Ulm on March 14, 1879, Albert embarked on a remarkable journey filled with curiosity, challenges, and groundbreaking insights.

From his early years as a curious child fascinated by simple toys and natural phenomena to his struggles and triumphs in school, we'll explore how Albert's unique way of thinking paved the way for extraordinary discoveries. As Albert's curiosity deepened, he asked bold questions that challenged the very foundations of physics.

Join me as we unravel the mysteries of Albert Einstein's life—his unconventional ideas, his passion for knowledge, and his unwavering belief in the power of imagination. Through Albert's story, we'll learn valuable lessons about perseverance, creativity, and the joy of exploring the wonders of science.

Whether you're a young explorer curious about the universe or someone seeking inspiration from a legendary figure, this book invites you to embark on an unforgettable adventure. Let's follow in Albert Einstein's footsteps and discover the boundless possibilities that await those who dare dream and question the world around them. Get ready to be inspired, amazed, and empowered by Albert Einstein's remarkable life and legacy!

A Curious Kid

Once upon a time, in the small German city of Ulm, a baby boy named Albert was born on March 14, 1879. His parents, Hermann and Pauline Einstein were overjoyed to welcome their new son into the world. Little did they know this curious and lively child would one day change the way we understand the universe.

From the moment he could toddle around, Albert showed a keen interest in the world around him. His eyes sparkled with wonder as he played with simple toys, but his favorite was a tiny compass. Albert was captivated by the way the needle always pointed north. "Why does it do that?" he wondered, setting the stage for a lifetime of questioning.

As Albert grew older, his curiosity only deepened. He would spend hours watching leaves float down a stream, wondering why they moved as they did. His mind was always buzzing with questions, like a bee flitting from flower to flower.

In school, Albert's teachers quickly noticed that he was different from the other children. While some subjects bored him, like grammar and history, he was enthralled by mathematics and science. Albert's classmates didn't always understand his ideas, but that didn't bother him. He preferred to explore the world at his own pace, dreaming of riding on a beam of light or chasing after invisible forces.

At home, Albert's family nurtured his curiosity. His parents gave him books on science and mathematics, which he devoured eagerly. They encouraged his interests and allowed him to tinker with simple experiments in their cozy house.

Young Albert's childhood was filled with wonder and discovery. He dreamed of solving the mysteries of the universe and couldn't wait to grow up and explore the world of science even further.

Little did Albert know that his insatiable curiosity and boundless imagination would one day lead him to become one of the greatest scientists of all time, changing our understanding of space, time, and everything in between. As we journey through Albert's life, we'll discover how his questions and ideas shaped the course of history. And perhaps, like Albert, we'll be inspired to ask our own questions and dream our own dreams of discovery.

Finding His Voice

When Albert was a young child, he faced a challenge that made him different from other kids his age. While most children learned to talk quickly and easily, Albert's journey with speech was slower and more challenging.

As a toddler, Albert struggled to form words and express himself. His parents noticed that he was not speaking as fluently as other children his age. This worried them, but his mother, Pauline, believed in her son's abilities and encouraged him to keep trying.

Albert's slow development in speech didn't stop him from exploring the world around him. Instead of using words, he relied on observations and gestures to communicate. He was a keen observer, always watching and listening intently to the world unfolding around him.

Despite the initial setbacks with speech, Albert's mind was sharp and curious. He soaked up knowledge like a sponge and was particularly fascinated by the mysteries of numbers and patterns. Even without speaking much, he found ways to express his ideas through drawings and experiments.

As Albert grew older, he began to catch up with his peers in speech. His thoughts were complex and profound, and he needed time to find the right words to articulate them. When he did speak, people were often amazed by the depth of his insights.

Albert's slow development in speech taught him the value of patience and perseverance. He learned to trust his unique way of thinking and expressing himself, paving the way for his future as a brilliant scientist and thinker.

The Mysterious Compass

Albert loved to explore the world around him and was always full of questions. One day, when Albert was just a child, his father gave him a simple yet intriguing gift—a compass.

The compass was a small, round device with a needle that always pointed in the same direction—toward the North. Little Albert was captivated by this magical object. He would hold the compass in his hand, watching in amazement as the needle obediently turned and pointed northward, seemingly without any strings attached.

"Father, why does the needle always point in one direction?" Albert asked with wide-eyed wonder.

His father explained that the compass needle was responding to the Earth's magnetic field, which always points towards the magnetic North Pole. But for young Albert, this answer only sparked more questions.

Albert spent hours studying the compass, trying to understand the invisible forces that made it work. He wondered why the needle didn't move up, down, or sideways but always aligned itself northward. His fascination with the compass sparked a lifelong curiosity about the mysteries of nature and how things worked.

As Albert grew older, he carried the memory of that enchanted compass with him. The experience of holding such a simple yet profound object left a lasting impression on his young mind, igniting a passion for science and discovery.

School Days

As Albert grew older, it was time for him to go to school and continue his journey of learning. He attended school first in Germany and later in Switzerland. But school wasn't always easy for Albert because he liked to think about things in his own special way.

In class, Albert's mind often wandered as he daydreamed about the mysteries of the universe. While other students followed the rules, Albert liked to question everything. Sometimes, his teachers didn't understand his unconventional way of thinking.

Albert found some subjects boring, like grammar and history, but he absolutely loved math and science. He enjoyed solving puzzles and figuring out how things worked. Even though the school had its challenges, Albert's passion for learning continued to grow.

Despite his struggles with traditional schooling, Albert's teachers recognized his intelligence and unique perspective. They saw that he had a special way of looking at the world, even if it was different from what they were used to.

Throughout these school years, Albert's curiosity and determination to understand the mysteries of nature only deepened. Little did he know his unconventional thinking and love for math and science would lead him to amazing discoveries in the years to come.

Albert's story reminds us that it's okay to think differently and ask questions. Sometimes, the most extraordinary discoveries come from those who dare to see the world in a new light. As we follow Albert on his journey, let's keep our minds open and our curiosity alive, just like he did. Who knows what wonders we might uncover when we think outside the box and embrace our unique ways of understanding the world?

Challenging Authority

Albert Einstein was a brilliant thinker, even as a young student. He had a habit of questioning everything around him, including his teachers' explanations. While other students followed the rules, Einstein preferred to explore topics that interested him, even if they weren't part of the school curriculum.

In school, Einstein often clashed with his teachers because he didn't accept things at face value. He wanted to understand the reasons behind scientific principles and theories. When his teachers presented information, Einstein would challenge them with his own ideas and perspectives.

Einstein's independent thinking sometimes got him into trouble, but it also led to profound insights. He questioned traditional teaching methods and wasn't afraid to express his opinions, even when they went against the mainstream.

One famous story from Einstein's school days involves a disagreement with his physics teacher over the speed of light. The teacher insisted that light traveled at a constant speed, but Einstein questioned whether this was true in all circumstances. This early skepticism foreshadowed his later theories of relativity.

Despite facing criticism from authority figures, Einstein's determination to think for himself and follow his intellectual curiosity ultimately led him to revolutionize physics with his groundbreaking theories.

University Years

When Albert turned 21, he embarked on an exciting new adventure—university! He enrolled at the Swiss Federal Institute of Technology (ETH) in Zurich, Switzerland, to study physics. This marked the beginning of an important chapter in Albert's life, where he could delve deeper into the subjects that fascinated him.

At university, Albert was like a sponge, soaking up knowledge from his professors and books. He spent countless hours in the library, pouring over texts on mathematics and physics, eager to understand the secrets of the universe. One topic that particularly captivated him was the behavior of light—how it moved, reflected, and interacted with matter.

During his university years, Albert began to develop his own ideas and theories about the fundamental workings of nature. He pondered profound questions: What is time? How does space bend and stretch? These early musings were the seeds of the groundbreaking theories that would later make him famous.

Albert's professors quickly recognized his keen intellect and passion for physics. While some of his classmates stuck to conventional thinking, Albert wasn't afraid to challenge established theories and explore unconventional concepts. His professors admired his curiosity and encouraged him to pursue his ideas.

As Albert progressed through his studies, he started to stand out among his peers. He engaged in spirited discussions, sharing his insights and debating theories with others. Albert's time at university was not just about learning facts—it was about nurturing his creativity and fostering his independent thinking.

By the time Albert completed his university education in 1905, he was on the brink of something extraordinary. The seeds of his revolutionary ideas had taken root, ready to blossom into theories that would reshape our understanding of the cosmos.

Annus Mirabilis

In the year 1905, something truly extraordinary happened—it was Albert Einstein's "miraculous year"! This special period would forever alter the landscape of physics and challenge our fundamental understanding of the universe.

During this remarkable time, Albert, a young physicist working as a patent examiner in Switzerland, accomplished something extraordinary. He published not just one but several revolutionary papers that sent shockwaves through the world of science.

One of these groundbreaking papers introduced the Special Theory of Relativity—a theory that completely transformed our perception of time, space, and motion. Albert proposed that the speed of light in a vacuum is constant and does not change, regardless of the speed of the observer. This meant that time and space were not as fixed and absolute as people once thought.

According to Albert's theory, time can actually slow down or speed up depending on how fast an object is moving relative to someone else. This mind-bending concept challenged centuries-old ideas about the nature of reality and set the stage for a new era in physics.

But that's not all! Albert's most famous equation, $E=mc^2$, also emerged during this miraculous year. This equation revealed a profound truth: that mass (m) and energy (E) are interconnected. It showed that a small amount of mass could be converted into a large amount of energy and vice versa. This discovery had profound implications for understanding the inner workings of atoms and ultimately led to the development of nuclear energy.

Albert's ideas were not immediately accepted by everyone. Some scientists found them difficult to grasp at first. However, as more experiments and observations supported Albert's theories, they gained widespread recognition and forever altered the course of physics.

Albert Einstein's "miraculous year" of 1905 marked the beginning of his ascent to scientific fame. His bold ideas challenged conventional wisdom, inspiring generations of scientists to rethink the nature of the cosmos.

The Equation $E=mc^2$

In the world of science, one of the most remarkable discoveries came from Albert Einstein's brilliant mind. He unveiled an extraordinary equation that transformed our understanding of energy and matter. This equation, known as $E=mc^2$, revealed a fascinating secret about the universe.

Imagine a simple block of wood sitting on a table. It might seem like an ordinary object, but according to Einstein's incredible equation, even this block of wood contains an enormous amount of hidden energy.

Let's break down what this equation means:

- E stands for energy.
- m stands for mass, which is the amount of "stuff" that makes up an object.
- c represents the speed of light, which is a very big number—about 300,000 kilometers per second!

Einstein's equation tells us that energy (E) is equal to the mass (m) of an object multiplied by the speed of light squared (c^2). This means that even a small amount of mass can be converted into a tremendous amount of energy, as shown by the famous equation.

Now, how does this apply to stars like the sun? Well, inside the sun's core, hydrogen atoms come together to form helium through a process called nuclear fusion. During this fusion, a tiny amount of mass is transformed into a huge amount of energy, which is why the sun shines so brightly and gives us light and warmth.

But Einstein's equation doesn't just explain stars—it also helps us understand nuclear energy. When atoms split (nuclear fission) or fuse together (nuclear fusion), a small amount of mass is converted into a large amount of energy. This principle is the basis for nuclear power plants and even atomic bombs.

Albert Einstein's discovery of $E=mc^2$ has had a profound impact on our understanding of the universe. It shows us that matter and energy are interconnected—they can transform into each other under certain conditions.

So, the next time you marvel at the sun's brilliance or hear about nuclear power, remember Albert Einstein and his amazing equation. It's a reminder of the incredible secrets hidden within the ordinary objects around us, waiting to be uncovered by curious minds like Einstein's.

Family and Career

From 1905 to 1914, Albert Einstein's life took on new dimensions. In 1903, he married Mileva Maric, a fellow physicist he met during his university studies. Together, they shared a deep passion for science and engaged in stimulating discussions about the mysteries of the universe.

As a family man, Albert cherished his role as a father to their two sons, Hans Albert and Eduard. Despite his busy schedule as a physicist, Albert always made time to play with his children and inspire them with his love for learning.

Throughout this period, Albert held various positions at universities and scientific institutions. He was dedicated to advancing his research while also teaching and mentoring students. Albert's unconventional thinking and innovative ideas set him apart in the academic world, earning him respect and admiration among his peers.

Despite the demands of his career, Albert faced challenges balancing work and family life. He often had to move to different cities for his job, which sometimes meant being separated from Mileva and their children. However, Albert's passion for physics and his commitment to pushing the boundaries of scientific knowledge kept him focused and determined.

During these years, Albert continued to collaborate with other scientists and explore new frontiers in physics. His reputation as a brilliant thinker and visionary scientist continued to grow, laying the foundation for his future contributions to the field.

General Theory of Relativity

From 1915 to 1919, Albert Einstein embarked on an incredible journey to unravel the mysteries of gravity and spacetime.

Einstein's quest began with a profound realization: What if gravity wasn't just a force that pulls objects toward each other but rather a fundamental bending of the very fabric of space and time? This idea led him to develop the General Theory of Relativity, a revolutionary concept that would redefine our understanding of the universe.

Imagine a giant trampoline stretched out in space. When you place a heavy ball on the trampoline, it creates a dip—a curve—in the surface. According to Einstein's theory, this is similar to how mass bends spacetime. Planets, stars, and other massive objects create "dips" in spacetime, causing smaller objects like comets or spacecraft to follow curved paths around them.

Einstein's work on the General Theory of Relativity was no easy task. It required complex mathematics and imaginative thinking. He spent years refining his theory, exploring the intricate relationship between matter, energy, space, and time.

But Einstein's theory faced skepticism. Many scientists were skeptical of his bold ideas, and some thought they were too radical to be true. It wasn't until 1919, during a total solar eclipse, that Einstein's theory received a crucial confirmation.

During the eclipse, astronomers observed something extraordinary: the positions of stars near the sun appeared to shift due to the sun's gravity bending the path of light. This observation perfectly matched the predictions of Einstein's theory.

The confirmation of Einstein's theory during the solar eclipse of 1919 captured the world's attention. Overnight, Albert Einstein became a scientific celebrity, celebrated for his groundbreaking insights into the nature of the cosmos.

Einstein's General Theory of Relativity transformed our understanding of gravity. It revealed that gravity is not just a force acting at a distance but a fundamental property of spacetime itself—a dynamic, interconnected fabric that shapes the paths of objects in the universe.

Validating Einstein's Theory

After Albert Einstein shared his incredible theories of relativity with the world, scientists everywhere were eager to see if these ideas were true. They wanted to find evidence that could prove Einstein right!

One of the first exciting experiments happened during a solar eclipse in 1919. Scientists went on an expedition to observe the stars near the sun when the moon hid it. What they saw amazed them—the positions of the stars appeared to shift slightly because the sun's gravity was bending the path of light, just like Einstein had predicted! This discovery showed that massive objects like the sun could bend spacetime, proving Einstein's theory of general relativity.

Another important validation of Einstein's theory came from studying how light behaves near massive objects. According to Einstein's theory, light traveling near a star would lose energy and shift to a lower frequency due to the star's gravity. Scientists observed this phenomenon, called gravitational redshift, by studying the light emitted by stars. The observed redshift matched exactly with what Einstein had predicted, providing more evidence for the truth of general relativity.

Einstein's theory also helped explain the mysterious precession of Mercury's orbit around the sun. Mercury's orbit was slightly different from what classical physics predicted, but Einstein's theory accurately accounted for this by considering the curvature of spacetime caused by the sun's mass. Observations of Mercury's orbit confirmed Einstein's predictions, showing that general relativity was indeed correct.

But Einstein's theories didn't just stay in space—they had real-life applications, too! Scientists discovered that Einstein's ideas about time dilation (how time moves slower for objects moving at high speeds) were true. They tested this in particle accelerators, where fast-moving particles showed longer lifetimes than expected due to time dilation effects.

Did you know that Einstein's theories even helped make GPS (Global Positioning System) technology accurate? GPS satellites and receivers use precise calculations that consider both special and general relativity effects to determine positions on Earth accurately.

Through all these experiments and discoveries, Albert Einstein's theories of relativity stood strong and changed the way we understand the universe. They showed us that sometimes, the most imaginative ideas can turn out to be true! Einstein's legacy continues to inspire scientists to explore new frontiers and uncover the secrets of our amazing universe.

Nobel Prize and Aftermath

During the years from 1921 to 1932, Albert Einstein achieved a major milestone in his scientific career—he was honored with the Nobel Prize in Physics. This prestigious award recognized his groundbreaking work on the photoelectric effect, which showed that light behaves as particles (photons) when interacting with matter.

Receiving the Nobel Prize was a momentous occasion for Albert. It brought him widespread recognition and highlighted the importance of his contributions to physics. However, Albert's journey didn't stop there. He continued to push the boundaries of scientific knowledge and explore new frontiers in his field.

Meanwhile, the world around Albert was undergoing significant changes. The aftermath of World War I left deep scars, and Albert became a vocal advocate for peace and international cooperation. He believed in using science and reason to promote understanding and prevent future conflicts.

Amidst these turbulent times, Albert also experienced personal changes. His marriage to Mileva Maric came to an end, and he remarried Elsa Einstein, his cousin. Together, they faced the challenges of blending their families and navigating life in a world still recovering from the effects of war.

Despite the upheavals, Albert remained committed to his scientific pursuits. He explored new theories and attempted to unify the laws of physics. His quest for a "unified field theory" aimed to explain all the forces of nature within a single framework, combining his insights from relativity and quantum mechanics.

Rise of Nazism

During the years from 1933 to 1939, Albert Einstein faced one of the most challenging periods of his life as the political landscape in Germany underwent a dramatic transformation with the rise of Nazism.

As a person of Jewish heritage and a prominent intellectual known for his outspoken views against nationalism and anti-Semitism, Albert became a prime target of persecution by the Nazi regime. His scientific achievements and fame did not protect him from the escalating threats and harassment aimed at Jewish individuals in Germany.

In 1933, faced with increasing danger, Albert Einstein made the difficult decision to leave his homeland. He and his family fled Germany, seeking refuge abroad. They settled in the United States, where Albert was offered a position at the prestigious Princeton Institute for Advanced Study in New Jersey.

Albert's move to the United States marked a new chapter in his life and career. Princeton University provided him with a safe haven in which to continue his scientific research and academic pursuits. Despite the upheaval of leaving Germany behind, Albert found a welcoming community of scholars and researchers at Princeton, allowing him to focus on his work in physics.

During this period, Albert Einstein's contributions to science continued to flourish. He collaborated with other brilliant minds in the field of theoretical physics, contributing to groundbreaking research in quantum mechanics and cosmology. Despite the personal challenges and uncertainties of exile, Albert remained dedicated to advancing human knowledge and understanding.

Settling in a new country was not without its difficulties. Albert had to adjust to a different culture and way of life, learn English, and adapt to American customs. However, he found intellectual stimulation and camaraderie among his colleagues at Princeton, fostering a vibrant environment for scientific exploration.

Albert Einstein's escape from Nazi persecution and his subsequent relocation to the United States underscored his courage and resilience in the face of adversity. His unwavering commitment to intellectual freedom and human dignity left a lasting impact on the scientific community and beyond.

World War II and Atomic Bomb

During the years from 1939 to 1945, Albert Einstein confronted the grave challenges of World War II and the looming threat of nuclear weapons, which deeply troubled him due to his profound understanding of physics and the potential consequences of harnessing atomic energy for destructive purposes.

Albert Einstein, along with other leading scientists, recognized the theoretical possibility of using nuclear fission to create immensely powerful bombs. Concerned about the implications of such weapons, Albert became an outspoken advocate for peace and urged world leaders to exercise caution and restraint in their pursuit of nuclear technologies.

In 1939, Albert Einstein and physicist Leo Szilard co-signed a letter to President Franklin D. Roosevelt, warning of Germany's potential to develop atomic weapons and urging the United States to initiate its own research into nuclear fission. This letter ultimately contributed to the establishment of the Manhattan Project, a massive scientific endeavor aimed at developing nuclear weapons.

Despite his advocacy for nuclear disarmament, Albert Einstein did not directly participate in the Manhattan Project, as he was primarily focused on theoretical physics and did not wish to contribute to the development of weapons of mass destruction.

Throughout World War II, Albert also engaged in humanitarian efforts. He supported organizations that aided refugees fleeing persecution and provided assistance to those affected by the devastation of war. Albert believed strongly in the importance of international cooperation and understanding in preventing future conflicts.

After the war, Albert continued to advocate for peace and disarmament, emphasizing the need for global unity and the responsible use of scientific knowledge for the benefit of humanity.

Albert Einstein's concerns about nuclear weapons and his unwavering commitment to peace underscored his belief in the ethical responsibilities of scientists and intellectuals. His legacy as a scientific visionary and advocate for a better world continues to inspire generations to work towards a future free from the threat of nuclear conflict.

Later Years

During the years from 1945 to 1955, Albert Einstein's passion for exploring the mysteries of the universe continued to drive his work in theoretical physics, leading him on a quest for a unified field theory—a single framework that could explain all the fundamental forces of nature.

After the end of World War II and the devastating impact of the atomic bombings of Hiroshima and Nagasaki, Albert Einstein remained deeply concerned about the implications of nuclear weapons and the responsible use of scientific knowledge. He advocated for international cooperation and nuclear disarmament, emphasizing the importance of harnessing science for peaceful purposes.

Despite his advancing age, Albert remained intellectually active and engaged in scientific discourse. He continued to refine his theories of relativity and quantum mechanics, seeking to reconcile their seemingly disparate principles within a broader theoretical framework.

One of Albert's lifelong ambitions was to develop a unified field theory that could unify gravity with the other fundamental forces of nature—electromagnetism, weak nuclear force, and strong nuclear force. This ambitious pursuit occupied much of his later years, although he did not ultimately achieve his goal of formulating a complete and satisfactory unified theory.

In addition to his scientific endeavors, Albert Einstein also became increasingly vocal on social and political issues. He used his status as a public figure to advocate for civil rights, speaking out against racism and segregation in the United States. His moral convictions and commitment to justice resonated with people around the world.

Despite his celebrity status, Albert remained humble and approachable. He often corresponded with fellow scientists and admirers who sought his insights and advice. He valued collaboration and intellectual exchange, fostering a spirit of curiosity and discovery among colleagues and students alike.

Albert Einstein's later years were marked by a blend of scientific exploration, advocacy for peace and social justice, and personal reflection. His enduring legacy as a scientific visionary and humanitarian continues to inspire generations, reminding us of the profound impact that one individual's passion and convictions can have on the world.

Einstein's Relationships with Other Scientists

Albert Einstein wasn't just a brilliant scientist—he also had friendships and collaborations with other great minds of his time.

One of Einstein's close friends was Niels Bohr, a Danish physicist known for his work on atomic structure. Bohr and Einstein often had lively discussions about the strange world of quantum physics, which deals with tiny particles like atoms and electrons. They didn't always agree on everything; in fact, Einstein famously said, "God does not play dice with the universe," expressing his skepticism about certain aspects of quantum theory. Despite their differences, Bohr's ideas challenged Einstein to think deeply about the nature of reality on a very small scale.

Another influential scientist in Einstein's life was Max Planck, who was like a mentor to him. Planck's work on the behavior of light and matter laid the groundwork for Einstein's theory of light as particles (photons). Planck encouraged Einstein to pursue his ideas, even when they seemed unconventional.

Einstein also had interactions with Erwin Schrödinger, an Austrian physicist famous for his wave equation that describes the behavior of atoms and molecules. Schrödinger's work on quantum mechanics fascinated Einstein and challenged his views about how the universe operates at the smallest levels. Schrödinger's famous thought experiment involving a theoretical cat that could be both alive and dead (known as Schrödinger's cat) highlighted the bizarre and puzzling nature of quantum theory.

These relationships with Bohr, Planck, and Schrödinger were crucial for Einstein's development as a scientist. They pushed him to think differently and consider new possibilities. Even when they disagreed, these interactions helped Einstein refine his theories and contribute groundbreaking ideas to physics.

Through these friendships and collaborations, Einstein showed us that science isn't just about individual genius— it's also about teamwork, sharing ideas, and learning from one another. These relationships remind us that great discoveries often come from the collective efforts of many brilliant minds working together.

Personal Life and Hobbies

Albert Einstein's life was filled with fascinating interests and hobbies that provided balance and inspiration alongside his scientific endeavors.

Beyond his revolutionary work in physics, Albert had a profound passion for music. He was an accomplished violinist and found immense joy in playing classical pieces. Music served as a creative outlet for Albert, allowing him to express emotions and explore the beauty of harmony. Interestingly, Albert saw connections between the mathematical structure of music and the laws of physics, appreciating the intricate patterns that both disciplines shared.

Another beloved pastime of Albert was sailing. He cherished the tranquility of being on the water, navigating sailboats with a sense of adventure and freedom. Sailing provided Albert with a refreshing escape from the complexities of theoretical physics, allowing him to connect with nature and experience the exhilaration of exploring new horizons.

In addition to music and sailing, Albert Einstein was deeply engaged in philosophical inquiries. He pondered profound questions about the nature of reality, consciousness, and the universe. Albert's philosophical explorations often intertwined with his scientific pursuits, shaping his perspectives on the fundamental principles that govern the cosmos.

Despite his busy schedule and intellectual pursuits, Albert valued these hobbies as essential aspects of his life. They offered him moments of relaxation, creativity, and reflection, contributing to his holistic approach to understanding the world.

Albert Einstein's diverse interests and hobbies highlight the depth and richness of his character. They not only provided him with personal fulfillment but also fueled his intellectual curiosity and creativity, ultimately influencing his remarkable contributions to science and philosophy.

Legacy and Impact

Albert Einstein's influence on science and culture remains profound, touching both the realms of physics and popular imagination.

Albert's groundbreaking theories of relativity transformed our understanding of the universe. His Special Theory of Relativity introduced the concept that time and space are interconnected, challenging centuries-old notions of absolute space and time. The famous equation $E=mc^2$, derived during his "miraculous year" of 1905, revealed the equivalence of mass and energy, leading to revolutionary advancements in nuclear physics.

Beyond his scientific achievements, Albert Einstein's iconic image and distinctive appearance have made him a cultural icon. His unruly hair, often rumpled clothes, and thoughtful gaze have been immortalized in countless photographs and artworks. Interestingly, Albert's penchant for wearing the same style of clothing every day—a simple gray suit with no socks—reflected his desire to minimize unnecessary decisions and focus his energies on more important matters.

In popular culture, references to Albert Einstein abound. His name is synonymous with intelligence and innovation, often used to represent genius or unconventional thinking. Countless movies, television shows, and books feature characters inspired by Einstein's persona.

Despite his scientific fame, Albert Einstein remained humble and approachable. He had a playful sense of humor and enjoyed engaging in thought experiments and philosophical discussions with friends and colleagues. One famous anecdote recounts how Albert once said life is like riding a bicycle. To keep your balance, you must keep moving."

Albert's legacy extends beyond science into the realm of humanitarianism. He advocated for peace and social justice, using his platform to speak out against racism and oppression. Albert believed in the power of education and reason to promote understanding and harmony among people.

Today, Albert Einstein's enduring legacy serves as a testament to the transformative impact of curiosity, imagination, and perseverance. His life and work continue to inspire generations of scientists, thinkers, and dreamers, encouraging us to push the boundaries of knowledge and strive for a better world.

Einstein's Imagination and Thought Experiments

In Albert Einstein's world, imagination was the key to unlocking the secrets of the universe. He had a special way of thinking about things—not just with numbers and formulas but with vivid pictures in his mind.

Imagine this: Albert Einstein sitting at his desk, deep in thought. Instead of staring blankly at a piece of paper, he closes his eyes and begins to imagine himself riding on a beam of light. He wonders, "What would it be like to travel so fast that time itself slows down?" This simple thought experiment led him to develop the theory of relativity, which changed our understanding of space, time, and gravity.

Another time, Albert imagined two twins—one staying on Earth and the other zooming away in a rocket ship at incredible speed. He asked himself, "Would time pass differently for the twin in the rocket compared to the twin on Earth?" This playful idea helped him realize that time can stretch and bend depending on how fast you're moving.

Albert's imagination wasn't just about daydreaming. It was a powerful tool he used to solve complex problems. By picturing himself in unusual situations or looking at things from different angles, he could see things that others couldn't.

He believed that imagination was even more important than knowledge. To Albert, creativity and curiosity were the keys to unlocking new discoveries. He encouraged everyone to think outside the box and not be afraid to ask big questions.

Albert Einstein's imaginative approach to science continues to inspire people today. His ability to use thought experiments to explore the mysteries of the universe reminds us that sometimes, the most powerful tools we have are the ones inside our minds.

So, the next time you look up at the stars or wonder about the world around you, remember Albert Einstein and his extraordinary imagination. Who knows what amazing discoveries you might make when you let your imagination soar?

Curious Quotes and Fun Facts

In the world of Albert Einstein, there were many wise sayings that captured his unique perspective on life and science. One of his famous quotes was, "Imagination is more important than knowledge." This meant that creativity and the ability to dream up new ideas were crucial for making big discoveries, even more so than just memorizing facts.

Another intriguing quote from Einstein was, "The important thing is not to stop questioning. Curiosity has its own reason for existing." This emphasized the value of asking questions and seeking answers, as curiosity is what drives us to explore and learn more about the world around us.

Albert Einstein also compared life to riding a bicycle, saying, "To keep your balance, you must keep moving." This clever analogy reminded us that progress and growth require continuous effort and forward motion, just like pedaling to stay balanced on a bike.

Now, let's uncover some fun facts about Albert Einstein's life. Did you know that as a child, Albert was a late talker and had difficulty with language early on? However, he had a natural talent for mathematics and science, which eventually led him to become one of the greatest scientists in history.

Albert Einstein's iconic hairstyle wasn't just a fashion statement—it was a deliberate choice to save time. He believed that maintaining a simple hairstyle would allow him to focus more on his work and less on his appearance.

In 1952, Albert was offered the presidency of Israel, but he declined the honor, saying he didn't have the necessary skills for political leadership. Despite his brilliance in science, Albert preferred to focus on his research and advocacy for social justice.

Throughout his life, Albert Einstein was a passionate advocate for civil rights and equality. He spoke out against racism and discrimination, urging people to treat each other with respect and understanding.

These curious quotes and fun facts about Albert Einstein reveal a fascinating and multifaceted individual—a scientist, thinker, and humanitarian whose legacy continues to inspire generations to explore, question, and dream big.

Einstein's Universe Today

Imagine a world shaped by Albert Einstein's extraordinary ideas—a world where his theories continue to profoundly influence modern science and technology.

Albert Einstein's theories of relativity, both special and general, have had a transformative impact on our understanding of the universe. They provide the framework for studying everything from the behavior of light and gravity to the structure of space and time. Without Einstein's insights, many of today's scientific advancements would not be possible.

One remarkable example of Einstein's legacy in modern technology is the Global Positioning System (GPS). GPS relies on precise timing signals transmitted from satellites orbiting Earth. However, due to the satellites' high speed and the gravitational effects they experience, the effects of both special and general relativity must be accounted for in these calculations. Without Einstein's theories, GPS devices would quickly become inaccurate, highlighting the practical importance of his work in our daily lives.

Einstein's famous equation $E=mc^2$, which describes the equivalence of mass and energy, continues to be foundational in nuclear physics and astrophysics. It underpins our understanding of nuclear reactions, such as those occurring in the sun, and has led to advancements in nuclear energy and particle physics.

Beyond technology, Albert Einstein's influence extends into our approach to scientific inquiry and education. He emphasized the importance of curiosity and imagination in the pursuit of knowledge. Einstein's legacy encourages us to ask questions, challenge assumptions, and explore new frontiers of understanding.

Today, Einstein's ideas continue to inspire researchers and innovators across diverse fields of science and technology. His work serves as a testament to the power of human curiosity and creativity in unraveling the mysteries of the universe.

As we navigate through Einstein's universe today, let us embrace his spirit of exploration and discovery. By harnessing the legacy of this brilliant scientist, we can continue to push the boundaries of

knowledge and shape a future driven by
curiosity, innovation, and wonder.

CONCLUSION

As we come to the end of our journey through Albert Einstein's life, let us reflect on the incredible legacy left behind by this visionary scientist. Albert's story teaches us valuable lessons about the importance of curiosity, perseverance, and the boundless power of imagination.

Throughout his life, Albert Einstein challenged conventional thinking and dared to explore the unknown. His theories of relativity revolutionized our understanding of space, time, and energy, paving the way for countless scientific advancements that continue to shape our world today.

But beyond his scientific contributions, Albert's story is a testament to the transformative impact of curiosity and passion. He reminds us that asking questions and embracing our curiosity can lead to unexpected discoveries and profound insights.

As we look back on Albert's life, let us carry forward his spirit of exploration and innovation. Let us nurture our own curiosity, follow our dreams, and never be afraid to think differently.

Whether you aspire to be a scientist, an artist, or a dreamer, remember that the journey of discovery begins with a single question. Like Albert Einstein, let us continue to seek answers, explore new horizons, and strive to make the world a better place.

Thank you for joining me on this inspiring adventure through the life of Albert Einstein. May his story inspire you to reach for the stars and embrace the wonders of the universe with an open heart and a curious mind. As Albert once said, "The important thing is not to stop questioning." So, let's keep questioning, exploring, and dreaming—because the greatest discoveries are yet to come.

Made in the USA
Monee, IL
27 November 2024

71441983R00056